The Official
RANGERS
Annual 2009

Written By Douglas Russell

A Grange Publication

© 2008. Published by Grange Communications Ltd., Edinburgh, under licence from Rangers Football Club. Printed in the EU.

ISBN 978-1-906211-43-1

Photography by Lynne Cameron
Picture Research Aileen Wilson

£6.99

Contents

AUGUST

For the opening league fixture, Walter Smith's side headed north to the Tulloch Stadium and a game against Inverness CT. Barry Ferguson, leading by example, not only bossed the midfield but also scored twice in a comprehensive 3-0 win. Second half substitute Nacho Novo's goal - a super right foot drive from the edge of the area — was sandwiched between the Captain's impressive double before a record crowd of 7,711 at this ground.

At home the following week, St Mirren offered resistance for much of the game but second period goals from Ferguson (following good approach play by both Alan Hutton and Lee McCulloch) and debutant striker Daniel Cousin secured all three points for top-of-the-table Rangers.

With more goals at Ibrox than the day's other four SPL games combined — a total of nine compared to eight elsewhere - Rangers went on a scoring spree against Falkirk, burying no less than seven past on-loan Newcastle goalkeeper Tim Krul. Both Daniel Cousin, who started the rout with a second minute strike, and Jean-Claude Darcheville (a substitute replacement for Cousin late in the game) each claimed a double. Steven Whittaker, Kris Boyd and Kirk Broadfoot also netted as the Light Blues romped to a 7-2 win and a magnificent seven for the first time since the home clash with St Mirren back in November 2000.

Powerhouse Darcheville made another substitute appearance seven days later at Rugby Park but this time the Frenchman, rapidly becoming a real favourite down Govan way, claimed the winner in a hard-fought 2-1 victory over Kilmarnock after Invincible cancelled out DaMarcus Beasley's second half opener.

SEPTEMBER

Just hours after completing his transfer from Kilmarnock, Steven Naismith made his Rangers debut to the sound of a standing ovation near the end of the 4-0 home win over Gretna, the previous season's First Division champions. A Kris Boyd free-kick, headers from central defenders Andy Webster and Carlos Cuellar plus a Collin own goal did all the damage to the SPL newcomers.

Smith's men were 2-0 behind at Tynecastle by the time Barry Ferguson took to the field as a second period replacement for Amdy Faye. Making an almost immediate impact, the Club Captain won a penalty (from Neilson's trip) that Cousin duly converted. At the end of the day, however, Hearts deservedly took all three points as Rangers unbeaten league sequence came to an end after this 4-2 reversal.

Following a sluggish first forty-five by the men in blue against Aberdeen at Ibrox, Lee McCulloch's glorious 25 yard volley changed the complexion of the game early in the second half. The second that afternoon was - in its own way - just as impressive when Naismith netted from a tight angle following his surge into the visitors' area. Substitute Kris Boyd completed the scoring that took Rangers back to the top of the table following Celtic's Easter Road defeat earlier in the day.

At Fir Park, the Light Blues found themselves in real danger of losing consecutive away SPL encounters after Mark McGhee's Motherwell took a first half lead through Porter. Rangers responded well after the break, however, and, following Kris Boyd's equaliser from the penalty spot twenty-five minutes before the end, continued to press without ever quite managing to find a winner in Lanarkshire.

OCTOBER

With Boyd employed as a lone striker, the team disappointed against Hibernian at Ibrox. Full-back David Murphy's second half headed goal for the visitors was the difference between the sides.

Nacho Novo was handed only his second SPL start of the season for the first Old Firm clash of the campaign. As always, the gutsy Spaniard did all that was asked of him – his superb 'whirling dervish' display included two goals (one in each half) in an emphatic 3-0 victory. Following Alan Hutton's cross into the box, Rangers first of the afternoon was headed home by Novo after he reacted far quicker than the Celtic back line. Man-of-the-match Barry Ferguson claimed the second some ten minutes after the break when he spun in the box to hit a right foot shot past Boruc. A penalty conversion by Novo (after Adam was brought down) completed a more than satisfactory day's work for Walter and his men.

The side's less than perfect away form continued at Tannadice with a 2-1 defeat at the hands of Dundee United. Although Daniel Cousin's second half penalty had cancelled out Wilkie's earlier opener, Barry Robson hit the winner with the second spot kick of the afternoon.

NOVEMBER

Kris Boyd's early opener against Inverness CT at Ibrox – he struck in less than one minute – was the player's eighth goal in eleven starts. Carlos Cuellar's looping header in the second period made sure of all three points against Craig Brewster's dogged Highland outfit.

At Westfield, Cuellar again headed home but this time to open the scoring in the clash with Falkirk. After Jean-Claude Darcheville had increased Rangers lead early in the second period, Falkirk netted courtesy of substitute Moutinho before Allan McGregor was called into action and produced two good stops as the home side pressed hard. Kris Boyd wrapped it up with a poacher's goal right at the end (3-1) for the team's first away win in the SPL since August.

DECEMBER

Darcheville took his season's tally to five when he netted right at the beginning of the encounter against Kilmarnock at Ibrox. In the second half, Steven Whittaker (recalled to the team at left-back) made doubly sure and took the breath away with a stunning strike from the edge of the box after cutting inside two defenders.

It took a goalkeeping howler to ensure all three points in the home league encounter with Hearts after Lee McCulloch's early opener had been cancelled out by Velicka's headed leveller after the break. Then, close to the end of the game in a crowded area as Rangers pressed, Kurskis fumbled a catch, managing only to force the ball over his own line and gift victory.

Against Aberdeen, it really should have been five league wins in a row following a typically fiery Pittodrie encounter. Rangers, despite their numerical disadvantage after Lee McCulloch's first half dismissal, dominated from start to finish and took the lead with a Charlie Adam goal. Even although Miller equalised just before the interval, Smith's men continued to impress for the rest of the game but failed to convert their superiority into goals.

Motherwell's attack-minded policy ensured an engrossing Boxing Day clash in Glasgow but Daniel Cousin's low strike (late in the first half) set the Light Blues on the road to victory. Following a Quinn leveller for the visitors, an own goal by Porter calmed the crowd's post-Christmas nerves before substitute Kris Boyd hit a late third just to make sure.

The Easter Road victory that followed was undoubtedly one of the club's best league performances of the campaign so far. Although the final 2-1 score suggested a close contest, this was not a true reflection of the gulf between the two teams on the day. Early on in the first period, Steven Naismith opened the scoring, taking advantage of Chris Burke's inviting low cross. The goal of the game, however, belonged to Daniel Cousin who rifled home a glorious left foot shot from the edge of the box early in the second half before Hibernian claimed a consolation right at the end.

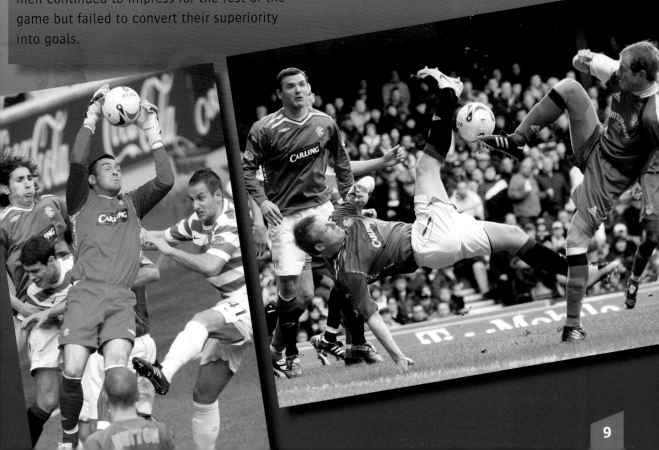

JANUARY

Following the cancellation of the Old Firm clash due to the tragic death of Motherwell captain and former Celt Phil O'Donnell, Rangers first game of 2008 was the 2-0 home win over Dundee United - a victory that saw Rangers return to the top of the table. Chris Burke, architect of both first half goals, provided pinpoint crosses into the box for, firstly, Naismith and then Ferguson to head home past keeper McLean. Barry Ferguson sported a special armband during the game as a tribute to the memory of O'Donnell whose funeral had taken place the previous day.

Rangers then hit the road with consecutive away fixtures to Gretna and Inverness. At Fir Park, Smith's men recorded a 2-1 win despite not being at their best. A volleyed finish by Ferguson just prior to the break and a goal from the tightest of angles by Cousin fifteen minutes before the final whistle (after Gretna had equalised at the start of the second period) meant that Rangers now enjoyed a four point advantage at the top following this hard-fought victory.

The team reached an impressive total of nine wins and a draw from their last ten league games following the 1-0 win over Inverness CT at the Tulloch Stadium in the Highlands. Even though it was something of another below-par performance, second half substitute Jean-Claude Darcheville's goal right at the end of the ninety minutes ensured another three crucial points in the championship race.

Against St Mirren at Ibrox, Chris Burke claimed his first Rangers goal since Walter Smith's return as Manager before the visitors were reduced to ten men following the dismissal of defender Haining. Subsequent goals from Steven Whittaker (a double left foot drive in the first half and a right foot strike in the second) and Kris Boyd ensured a comfortable 4-0 win. Incidentally defensive veteran David Weir, at the mature age of 37, made his 50th appearance for the Club in this game.

FEBRUARY

A Kris Boyd free kick midway through the first period – hit hard and low through an inviting hole in the Falkirk defensive wall – was all that separated the sides before substitute Steven Naismith claimed a second in the last minute of the home clash with John Hughes' side. For the visitors, Austrian keeper Olejnik caught the eye with more than one impressive save thus keeping the score at a respectable level.

By the end of the 2-0 away victory over Kilmarnock, the team had recorded their eighth successive clean sheet. Indeed, a playing time of 12 hours and 44 minutes in all competitions had lapsed since Gretna's Kenny Deuchar hit the back of the Rangers net in mid-January. A Carlos Cuellar header and a Kris Boyd penalty in the first and second half respectively continued Rangers fine run of form. For the record, it was Boyd's 16th goal from just 18 starts this season as well as his ninth goal in nine games against Kilmarnock, his former side.

Goals from Cousin, Naismith, Burke and Boyd guaranteed maximum points when relegation-threatened Gretna provided the opposition for another Sunday SPL clash. Although a late double from Kenny Deuchar obviously took some icing off the cake at Ibrox, it was not nearly enough to dampen the spirits on the day that Manager Walter Smith celebrated his 60th birthday, secure in the knowledge that his side was still involved on all four fronts in four separate domestic and European competitions.

In sharp contrast to the last visit to Tynecastle, Rangers totally dominated the capital clash against Hearts, scoring four goals without reply. Jean-Claude Darcheville and his interval replacement Nacho Novo both hit doubles on the night that Christian Dailly (a starting debut) and on-loan Northern Ireland international Steven Davis both impressed in midfield for a side full of flair and invention. Incidentally, the final goal of the night was from Novo with an audacious flick from the inside of his right boot that evaded Banks between the posts. Rangers had now recorded a 10th consecutive SPL win for the first time since 2003.

MARCH

Although Aberdeen impressed during the early stages of the initial league clash in March - and indeed took the lead via Lovell - Rangers responded well and equalised before the break when Christian Dailly fired home (from a Charlie Adam corner) with an emphatic side-footed, first-time volley. It was midfielder Adam himself who claimed his side's second with a well-placed glancing header from Kirk Broadfoot's cross into the box before Kris Boyd, from the penalty spot, made it 3-1 near the end.

Rangers then secured a 12th successive SPL victory in a fixture when their 100th strike in 50 games was also recorded. Against Hibernian at Ibrox, it was Jean-Claude Darcheville who opened the scoring just before the break when he drilled home a glorious right foot shot from a tight angle following a defence-splitting pass from Sasa Papac. Nacho Novo (Darcheville's second half replacement) hit the second with a low drive from 12 yards before Shiels pulled one back right at the end for a final score of 2-1 to the league leaders.

In many ways, Kevin Thomson could not have chosen a more ideal moment to score his first goal for the Club - it was the winning strike in the second Old Firm clash of the campaign. Celtic, to be fair, had threatened on more than one occasion early on, but following precise close interplay between Jean-Claude Darcheville and Thomson just before the break, the midfielder stroked home for the only goal of a pulsating ninety minutes. Although this was surely the game's defining moment, Allan McGregor's superb save from a fierce Hinkel drive in the second period is also worth recalling as it was goalkeeping of the very highest standard.

APRIL

At Tannadice (three days after playing Sporting Lisbon at the quarter-final stage of the UEFA Cup competition), Rangers came from behind three times in an enthralling 3-3 draw. Goals from David Weir (his first for the club), Nacho Novo and Kris Boyd ensured the point that extended the Club's lead at the top to seven following Celtic's home defeat to Motherwell the previous day. Despite being labelled defensive in certain quarters, Walter Smith's side had now recorded 73 league goals – at this stage of the season, more than any other side in the SPL.

The Light Blues suffered their first SPL defeat since the end of October when a late Jan Vennegoor of Hesselink goal secured a 2-1 win for Celtic in the penultimate Old Firm joust. Second half substitute Nacho Novo had earlier cancelled out Nakamura's opener but 10-man Rangers (Carlos Cuellar had been dismissed for handling a net bound shot) were cruelly denied right at the death, failing just by seconds to secure a crucial league point.

Back at Celtic Park just eleven days later, Carlos Cuellar, Allan McGregor, Lee McCulloch, Kevin Thomson, Chris Burke and Steven Naismith were all missing, either injured or suspended. Despite falling behind to an early strike from McDonald, Rangers hit back with headed goals by David Weir and Daniel Cousin, both from Steve Davis corners. McDonald then made it 2-2 just before the break. A Weir injury early in the second half was another blow - Rangers now had a rather unlikely central defensive partnership of Christian Dailly and Amdy Faye – and the afternoon's misery was complete when Robson hit the winner for Celtic from the penalty spot following a Kirk Broadfoot foul on McDonald.

MAY

Although both sides gave their all in an engrossing clash, there was nothing to separate Rangers and Hibernian at Easter Road and the teams had to settle for a point apiece following the 0-0 draw. To be crowned champions, Rangers now had to win all five of their remaining league games assuming Celtic proved victorious in their two remaining fixtures.

Against Motherwell in Glasgow three days later, another stalemate loomed large before Barry Ferguson won the game with a wonderful strike. Following a Steve Davis corner with less than twenty minutes to go, the Captain controlled with one touch before angling a tremendous hook shot into the far top corner. Ibrox erupted, acknowledging a goal fit to win any game.

Nacho Novo produced another man-of-the-match display in the home clash with Dundee United. His two goals in the first period – a close range header and wonderful left foot dipping volley from the edge of the box – set Rangers on the road to an eventual 3-1 win. In a controversial second half, de Vries pulled one back for the visitors before substitute Jean-Claude Darcheville netted right at the end following a free-flowing move that involved both Novo and Ferguson.

For Rangers 65th game of the season, the team headed for Fir Park to face a Motherwell side that had just clinched a UEFA Cup spot for 2008/2009. Despite taking the lead via Christian Dailly (a headed goal following Kirk Broadfoot's 40 yard ball into the penalty area), Porter's second half equaliser meant that two crucial points had been dropped to Celtic's obvious advantage. Incidentally, this was just the first of four games – three SPL fixtures and the Scottish Cup final – that the side had to play in the space of just one week!

Two days later at Love Street against St Mirren, Kris Boyd (with his 23rd goal of the campaign) opened the scoring in just three minutes when he bundled home Kirk Broadfoot's delivery across the box. Jean-Claude Darcheville then struck twice with a goal in each half to ensure a comprehensive 3-0 win. Both Rangers and Celtic now had 86 points apiece with one game remaining but Gordon Strachan's side had a better goal difference by four. The ultimate destination of the 2007/08 SPL flag would therefore be decided three days later when Rangers travelled north to Pittodrie to play Aberdeen and Celtic faced Dundee United at Tannadice.

Sadly, it was not to be for Rangers and a battle weary side – this was game number 67 of the season remember, as well as their 8th game in 22 days - lost 2-0 whilst Celtic registered a 1-0 win. Obviously that ultimate disappointment at the end of a long and winding road was hard to take, but in the clear light of an objective day, the fans were more than thankful, knowing that Walter's warriors had given their all over many months in the pursuit of glory.

Long after the final whistle, Hampden was still bouncing.

CIS Insurance Cup Campaign

Rangers progressed to the quarter-final stage of the CIS Insurance Cup competition after a comfortable 4-0 win over East Fife (conquerors of St Mirren in the previous round) at East End Park. Captain for the night Kris Boyd claimed a double - his 50th and 51st goals for the club – with both Nacho Novo and Carlos Cuellar also scoring.

Fir Park against Motherwell is never an easy game but this potential hazard was overcome 2-1 thanks to goals from Novo (another opener to go with his strike in the previous round) and Boyd before Quinn netted a consolation for the home side right at the end. Rangers would now be back at Hampden for the first time since March 2005.

The semi-final clash with Hearts - who disposed of Celtic in the previous round - was fought-out on a bitterly cold January night in front of a brave crowd of nearly 32,000 spectators. Second half goals from Barry Ferguson (a tremendous left foot hook shot with his back to goal that was whipped past Banks into the corner of the net) and Jean-Claude Darcheville (a close finish following Chris Burke's slide-rule pass into the box) ensured an important return date for Walter's warriors at the National Stadium in mid-March.

Just three days after facing UEFA Cup opponents Werder Bremen in Germany, Rangers and Dundee United contested the final of the CIS Insurance Cup at Hampden in front of a crowd of just over 50,000 expectant fans. Craig Levein's side took the lead (via Hunt) after half an hour's play and the cup seemed to be heading north before the introduction of Kris Boyd with ten minutes play remaining. His subsequent equaliser – capitalising on a suicidal passback by Kerr – took the game into extra-time. Although Mark de Vries handed the advantage back to Dundee United with a fine strike, that man Boyd hauled Rangers back from the jaws of defeat once again when he headed home to make it 2-2. The subsequent penalty shootout was just as dramatic and – surprise, surprise – was decided by Kris Boyd when he netted with the very last spot-kick to secure victory 3-2 on penalties.

Rangers: McGregor, Broadfoot, Cuellar, Weir, Papac (Boyd), Dailly, Hemdani (Darcheville), Davis, Ferguson, Burke (Whittaker) and McCulloch.

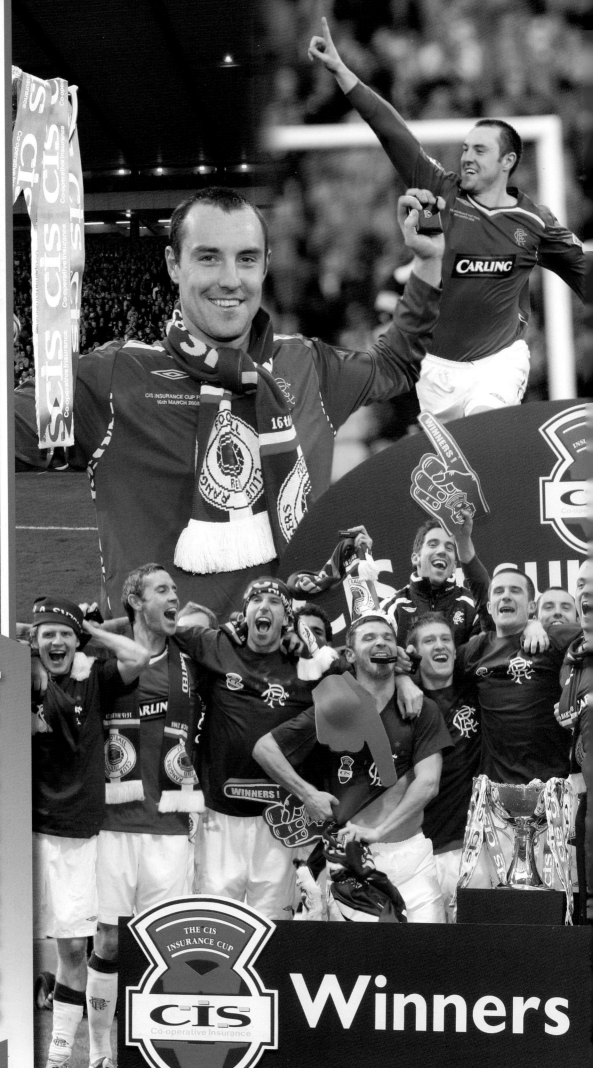

THE CIS
INSURANCE CUP

cis
Co-operative Insurance

Winners

008

NEIL ALEXANDER

After signing a three and a half year
contract at the end of January 2008, Edinburgh-born
Neil Alexander made his Rangers debut against Hibernian
at Easter Road in rather unlikely circumstances after Allan
McGregor's dismissal near the end of that early February
Scottish Cup tie. The keeper, signed from Ipswich, had
previously spent six years with English Championship side
Cardiff City, playing over 200 games for the Ninian Park
outfit. Following McGregor's unfortunate injury against
Celtic in the penultimate Old Firm clash of the SPL
campaign, Alexander proved to be a more than capable
deputy from then until the end of the season. He was
involved in two penalty shoot-outs – against both Partick
Thistle and Fiorentina at the semi-final stage of different
competitions – before the curtain finally fell on the
2007/08 period. Needless to say, his shoot-out save from
Fiorentina's Liverani during the game in Florence was one
of the key moments of the campaign.

KIRK BROADFOOT

Before arriving at the Club for
the start of the 2007/08 period, Kirk Broadfoot
had spent five years with St Mirren establishing
an impressive reputation as one of the best young
central defenders in Scotland. Circumstances
were such, however – Alan Hutton's January 2008
departure to Tottenham Hotspur being a major
consideration – that the player was employed by
manager Walter Smith as right full back for much of
the latter part of last season's domestic and European
tournaments. During that period, he seemed to
develop in both a physical and mental sense, making
the position very much his own. Following Rangers
final home game of 2007/08, the defender said:
'Doing the lap of honour was a dream come true
for me, having supported the Club all my life. It's
something I used to dream about as a wee boy.'

DAVID WEIR

On the day that Rangers played their final home league game last season - a 3-1 win over Dundee United - veteran defender David Weir (Walter Smith's first signing after returning as manager in January 2007) not only celebrated his 38th birthday but also another crucial SPL victory and three precious points in that never-ending championship race. There can be no doubt that his central defensive partnership with Carlos Cuellar was one of the main reasons for much of the Club's success both home and abroad during the various 2007/08 campaigns. Weir, a superb positional player and reader of the game, claimed his first-ever Rangers goal in the Champions League qualifying round clash with FK Zeta of Montenegro early on last season. He scored another twice last term – at Tannadice in April's 3-3 draw and at Celtic Park in the 3-2 Old Firm reversal the same month.

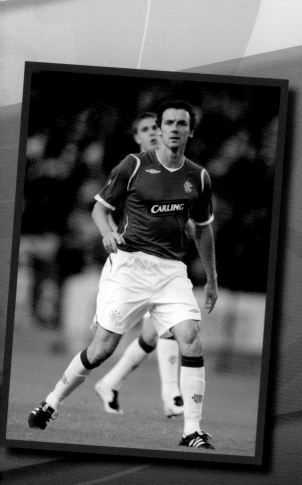

CHRISTIAN DAILLY

Dundee-born Christian Dailly was the youngest-ever player to appear for Dundee United when he made his first-team debut for the Tayside club in 1990. Following subsequent spells with both Derby County and Blackburn Rovers, the extremely versatile Dailly joined West Ham in January 2001. When the Hammers finished in seventh place at the end of Season 2001/02, he had played every minute of every league game. Last term, a few days after his Light Blue debut in the UEFA Cup clash against Panathinaikos in Greece, he claimed his first Rangers goal during the SPL fixture with Aberdeen at Ibrox when a side-footed volley cancelled out the visitors' early opener. Rangers went on to win 3-1.

SASA PAPAC

In the red-hot atmosphere of the Artemio Franchi Stadium in Florence at the beginning of May 2008, many Rangers fans were surprised to see Sasa Papac step forward to take one of his side's penalties in the shoot-out with Fiorentina. The fact that he did not disappoint at such a key moment that night really summed up his whole season in blue. One of three players signed from Austria Vienna by former manager Paul Le Guen, quiet man Papac had earlier survived career-threatening injuries after being involved in a head-on car crash in 2005. In addition to leg and head injuries, both his jaw and nose were shattered in the accident. Although previously recognised as a left-sided centre-half, Walter Smith utilised the player to great effect at left-back and in last season's glorious UEFA Cup campaign, Papac played in every match and was consistently impressive all the way to Manchester.

STEVEN WHITTAKER

After signing for Hibernian as a teenager from Hutchison Vale Boys Club – Kenny Miller was one of several players to take the same route – Steven Whittaker made his first team debut in the 1-0 home win over St Johnstone in May 2002. Later, under manager Tony Mowbray in Season 2004/05, he really came of age in the right-back role when the Edinburgh side clinched third place in the championship. Whittaker arrived at Ibrox for the start of the 2007/08 period (having agreed a five-year contract) and made his first appearance in the 7-2 win over Falkirk. He was one of five Rangers scorers that day. The player – equally at home in a variety of defensive/midfield positions – claimed another four goals last season with the pick of the bunch obviously being that memorable solo effort against Sporting Lisbon at the Estadio Jose Alvalade in Portugal when Rangers achieved a quite stunning UEFA Cup win.

STEVE DAVIS

Initially signed on a six month loan deal from Fulham in January 2008, midfielder Steve Davis, a boyhood Rangers fan, became Northern Ireland's youngest modern day captain for the game against Uruguay in May 2006. At club level, he had started his career with Aston Villa and quickly became a favourite with the supporters. Indeed, at the end of the 2005/06 campaign, he was honoured as Young Player of the Year, Fans' Player of the Year and Player of the Year! Then, in July 2007 for a fee of around £4 million, he joined Fulham where he was a regular until the departure of manager Lawrie Sanchez. Davis made his Rangers debut in the February UEFA Cup clash against Panathinaikos and, three weeks later, claimed his first Rangers goal in the same competition when Werder Bremen lost 2-0 at Ibrox. It was, of course, Davis who supplied the killer pass when Jean-Claude Darcheville opened the scoring on a famous night in Lisbon. As the Annual went to press Rangers were in negotiations to sign the midfielder on a long term contract.

KEVIN THOMSON

Walter Smith brought Kevin Thomson, the former Hibernian captain, to Rangers in January 2007. After an inevitable settling-in period, the combative midfielder soon hit his stride and ended the 2006/07 season in impressive form as the Ibrox side fought to secure their place in the Champions League for the following season. Although Thomson began last term in equally fine form – his partnership with Barry Ferguson at the heart of the midfield was crucial - injury was to play a major part in his season and the player was missing for several weeks from early January. His comeback game was the 1-0 Scottish Cup replay win over Hibernian in early March. At the end of that very same month, his name was on everyone's lips following an extremely important Ibrox clash when Rangers recorded their second Old Firm win of the campaign. Why? Quite simply, Thomson's first-ever goal for the Club was just enough to ensure another three crucial SPL points following Rangers 1-0 win that day.

CHARLIE ADAM

Midfielder Charlie Adam returned to Rangers for the 2006/07 campaign after having spent the whole of Season 2005/06 on-loan at St Mirren and ended that former period as very much a first-team regular with 14 goals to his name. That number, incidentally, meant that only top scorer Kris Boyd had netted more times. Last season, both appearances and goals were more limited with totals of 25 and four respectively. The player scored twice in the 2007/08 SPL fixtures – against Aberdeen on both occasions. Firstly, he claimed the opener at Pittodrie in late December (1-1) and, secondly, his glancing header was number two of three at Ibrox in the 3-1 win at the beginning of March. His two European goals came in the Champions League clashes with Stuttgart when Rangers won at Ibrox but lost at the Gottlieb Daimler Stadium. The strike in the former clash was, quite simply, one of the best goals of the season.

BARRY FERGUSON

Despite being not fully fit at various stages last season – he carried a restricting ankle injury for much of the latter part of the campaign – Barry Ferguson made an astonishing 60 starts (plus one substitute appearance) throughout the 2007/08 period. There can be no doubt that he played a true captain's part and never shirked the challenge as Rangers battled on all four fronts in search of both domestic and European silverware. On the very first day of the SPL season Ferguson, leading by example, scored twice in the 3-0 win over Inverness CT at the Tulloch Stadium. He netted an additional seven times last term including memorable strikes against Celtic in the league at Ibrox (3-0, 20.10.07) and Hearts in the CIS Insurance Cup at Hampden (2-0, 30.1.08). Late on in the race for championship glory, his winner in the home fixture with Motherwell (1-0, 7.5.08) was one of the goals of the season. A driving force right to the end of the season, Ferguson's man-of-the-match performances from 2007/08 are, however, simply too many to list.

LEE McCULLOCH

After being injured in a tackle with Paul Hartley during the penultimate Old Firm clash of 2007/08, it looked as if Lee McCulloch's season had come to a premature end but thankfully that was not the case and the player, despite being not fully match-fit, made a substitute appearance against Zenit St Petersburg in the UEFA Cup final. Less than two weeks later, he was in the starting line-up on Scottish Cup final day in late May. McCulloch joined Rangers from Wigan for the start of Season 2007/08 (having agreed a four-year deal) and made a total of 38 starts for the Ibrox men throughout that period. He scored seven goals in all competitions – three in the SPL, two in the Scottish Cup and two in the Champions League. Although his strike in the 2-0 home win over FK Zeta in the Champions League qualifying round was obviously important, his opener in the same tournament against Lyon at the Stade Gerland was a bit more special and one of the goals of the season.

CHRIS BURKE

Winger Chris Burke claimed his first Rangers goal since Walter Smith's return as manager of the Club in the comprehensive 4-0 win over St Mirren at Ibrox in late January 2008. Then, after scoring against Gretna in the 4-2 SPL win the following month, the Murray Park graduate hit the winner – a glorious left foot strike from fifteen yards – when Hibernian provided the opposition for a Scottish Cup replay in early March. Although this tournament provided another highlight for the player when he netted against First Division Partick Thistle in the quarter-final replay at Firhill (2-0, 13.4.08), Burke's most vivid memories of this competition will surely be for other reasons as he subsequently suffered severe ankle damage against St Johnstone during the semi-final stage at Hampden in April. With surgery successfully carried out in late May, the player is scheduled to be back in action for Rangers sometime during the winter of 2008.

JEAN-CLAUDE DARCHEVILLE

A favourite of the fans virtually from his first appearance in Rangers colours, Jean-Claude Darcheville is now in his second season with the Club. The Frenchman was impressive both home and abroad in 2007/08 as the Light Blues challenged on all fronts. In the SPL, after an appearance as substitute, he hit a double in the second home game of the campaign when seven goals demolished Falkirk. He came off the bench again for the next league game but this time his name was on the winner at Rugby Park when Rangers won 2-1. In total, his league tally of goals was twelve for the season including doubles in the clashes with Hearts at Tynecastle (4-0, 27.2.08) and St Mirren at Love Street (3-0, 19.5.08). Darcheville was particularly impressive filling the role of lone striker in Europe and, hardly surprisingly when considering the work rate involved, never completed a full ninety minutes prior to that date with destiny and Zenit St Petersburg in Manchester in May 2008. His goal away to Sporting Lisbon was marvellous in both build-up

DaMARCUS BEASLEY

During his time with PSV Eindhoven, USA international DaMarcus Beasley became the first American to play at the semi-final stage of the Champions League competition when PSV faced AC Milan during the 2004/05 period. The speedy winger claimed two goals for Rangers in that very tournament last season – the winner against FK Zeta in Podgorica (1-0, 7.8.07) and Rangers third of a most memorable evening in France when Lyon were tamed 3-0 at the beginning of October. Domestically, Beasley was also making his mark but then, at the end of November, he was badly injured during the Champions League 3-2 defeat in Stuttgart and his season seemed to be over. However, after appearing as a substitute late-on against St Mirren in the penultimate SPL fixture, the winger made the Scottish Cup final starting line-up five days later. His super display at Hampden included Rangers opener in the 3-2 win over Queen of the South.

NACHO NOVO

Never giving less than 100% to the cause every time he wears the blue, Nacho Novo naturally holds a special place in the hearts of all Rangers fans. Last season, in his second SPL start of the league campaign, he struck twice (one goal in each half) in the first Old Firm clash of the 2007/08 period when Celtic lost 3-0 at Ibrox. Novo netted another eight league goals last term, two of which came in the final home game when the player was man-of-the-match in the 3-1 win over Dundee United. His second that warm afternoon was a quite astonishing volley from the edge of the penalty area. Away from the domestic arena, the striker's two European goals last season were both crucial. Firstly, his last minute goal against Red Star at Ibrox in the Champions League qualifying round ensured Rangers place in the group stages and, secondly, his late equaliser in the Athens UEFA Cup clash with Panathinaikos meant a place in the last sixteen of the tournament. Although Novo missed the Scottish Cup final through suspension, he played his part earlier in the competition and scored at both the quarter and semi-final stage in the games with Partick Thistle and St Johnstone respectively.

KRIS BOYD

The top scorer at the Club again last season with his impressive 25 goals in 25 starts spread throughout all of the 2007/08 domestic tournaments - 14 in the SPL, six in the Scottish Cup and five in the CIS Insurance Cup competition. By comparison, he totalled 26 goals in the same tournaments during 2006/07. Although the Scot hit a hat-trick against East Stirlingshire in Rangers first Scottish Cup outing last term, it was in the final of the competition he really made his mark with a brace (including the winner) against Queen of the South at Hampden. Of course, at the same venue two months earlier, his late substitute appearance in the CIS Insurance Cup final famously changed the whole course of the game with Dundee United. The trophy seemed to be heading north before Boyd equalised right at the end. Into extra-time, he again pulled Rangers back from the brink after United had gone ahead for the second time in the game. Then, in the shoot-out, his decisive strike confirmed a 3-2 penalty win for Walter Smith's side and the first silverware of the campaign.

Rangers Annual Player of the Year

Carlos Cuellar – joint winner

In April 2008 when Carlos Cuellar was confirmed as SPL Player of the Year by sponsors Clydesdale Bank, the defender had featured in all but one of Rangers 55 games at that stage of the campaign. When the curtain finally fell at the end of that marathon season on Scottish Cup final day – by this time he was also the Scottish Football Writers' Association Player of the Year – the Spaniard had made 64 appearances, breaking the club record of 61 held jointly by Bobby Russell and Peter McCloy from Season 1978/79.

Although a gifted 1500 metre runner as a youngster, football was always going to be his chosen profession. Starting out with Spanish Tercera Division side Calahorra in 2000/01, Cuellar then moved to Segunda side Numancia (where he made over 60 appearances in the two seasons) before moving up a grade and joining La Liga outfit Osasuna. His four seasons there included a fourth place in the league for the 2004/05 period.

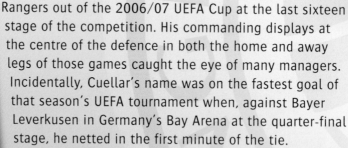

Two years later, the player was an integral part of the Osasuna side that knocked Rangers out of the 2006/07 UEFA Cup at the last sixteen stage of the competition. His commanding displays at the centre of the defence in both the home and away legs of those games caught the eye of many managers. Incidentally, Cuellar's name was on the fastest goal of that season's UEFA tournament when, against Bayer Leverkusen in Germany's Bay Arena at the quarter-final stage, he netted in the first minute of the tie.

His year in Glasgow was nothing less than a raging success – the first month ended as Clydesdale Bank Player of the Month for August - and the fans idolised him virtually right from the start. The player rarely put a foot wrong all season and his central defensive partnership with the veteran David Weir was a marriage made in blue heaven. At the other end of the park, Cuellar posed a more than considerable threat in the opposition box and, indeed, scored five times – home to both Gretna (4-0, 1.9.07) and Inverness CT (2-0, 3.11.07) and away to Falkirk (3-1, 24.11.07) and Kilmarnock (2-0, 17.2.08) in the SPL and, in the CIS Insurance Cup, away to East Fife (4-0, 26.9.07).

Although both the UEFA Cup and SPL campaigns ended without silverware, his towering displays at home and throughout the continent in both 2007/08 European competitions had earned plaudits from friend and foe alike.

Thanks for the memories

" His year in Glasgow was nothing less than a raging success – the first month ended as Clydesdale Bank Player of the Month for August - and the fans idolised him virtually right from the start. "

Who ? said that ?

1

'I thought the fans were unbelievable again. They were not swearing or shouting stupid things, they were just pushing their team forward and that's a great thing to see.'

'I didn't know that actually, but it's a pleasing stat considering we don't play any forwards.'

'When Rangers played in Bremen, I was in the stadium. I'm on the other side now, a fan like any other. The only difference being I played for Rangers and nobody can take that away from me.'

'I am over the moon. Everybody knows I am Rangers through and through. I am from a Rangers village and I managed to get as many tickets as I could.'

3

'They (Rangers) have found a way to win. It might not be beautiful but it has become impossible not to admire. They are on the verge of something magical – not in the way it has been achieved but in the distance travelled by a team that never looked like making this journey.'

4

2

5

'I think he'll be tucked up in bed by half past seven tonight because he's shattered. It's a real bonus, outwith the result and outwith the games we're playing, to get a wee bonus like that. And while it might seem like a wee bonus to us, to him it's everything.'

6

7

'I've always thought you were a great player and you proved it again tonight. You would fit perfectly into my team'

ANSWERS ON PG. 62

QUIZ: Headline News

Rangers made the following
football headlines last season.
What was the occasion?

THE BOYS ARE BACK IN TOWN
– Daily Mail, 7.1.08

HEART ON HIS SLEEVE
– Mail on Sunday, 6.1.08

RANGERS IN SEVENTH HEAVEN AFTER GOAL STROLL STUNS SAINTS
– Mail on Sunday, 27.1.08

A BRIEF FLASH OF BRILLIANCE
– Daily Mail, 17.1.08

STYLISH RANGERS SCORE PERFECT TEN
– The Herald, 28.2.08

A WIESE MAN BEARS GIFTS
– Daily Mail, 7.3.08

REMEMBER THE ALLANMO
– Daily Record, 14.3.08

NOBODY DOES IT BETTER
– Daily Mail, 17.3.08

ANSWERS ON PG. 62

KENNY MILLER

Kenny Miller returned to Rangers for a second spell with the Club prior to the start of Season 2008/09 after agreeing a three-year deal. Early in his senior career, the striker spent four years at Hibernian and was the club's top scorer at the end of the 1999/00 campaign. Then, in the summer of 2000, former Rangers manager Dick Advocaat brought Miller — by this time Scottish PFA Young Player of the Year — to Ibrox for a fee of £2 million. His first goal was during the 4-2 away win at Kilmarnock in August before he famously netted five times (a Scottish Premier League record) when St Mirren were crushed 7-1 three months later. After a season with the Light Blues, Miller then moved to English First Division outfit Wolves (initially on-loan) where he would spend five years. During that time, his 18 goals in the final six months of Season 2003/04 helped the club to gain promotion into the Premier League. Miller joined Celtic for the 2006/07 campaign and claimed crucial Champions League goals against FC Copenhagen and Benfica. He then moved south again (after a year in the east end of Glasgow) and joined newly promoted Derby County in the English Premiership. Last season, his winner against Newcastle in the 1-0 victory on 17 September was a bit special and was subsequently voted Goal of the Season by fans of the Rams. Following Derby's relegation, however, Walter Smith moved to bring the Scotland hitman back north and in due course he became a Rangers player yet again.

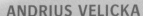

ANDRIUS VELICKA

Beginning his professional career at FKB Kaunas, striker Andrius Velicka would go on to play over 150 games for the Lithuanian side before joining Hearts on a loan deal for the start of the 2006/07 period. When 10-man Hearts drew 2-2 with Hibernian at Easter Road in the October Edinburgh derby that season, it was Velicka who scored both goals for his side. Then, the following January, he netted his first hat-trick in maroon when Stranraer were beaten 4-0 in the Scottish Cup. Last season, his first goal came in the early September 2-0 win over Motherwell at Fir Park before netting in consecutive fixtures; scoring against St Mirren at Love Street and Falkirk at Tynecastle. At the end of October, Velicka came off the bench in the CIS Insurance Cup quarter final clash at Celtic Park to claim both goals in a famous 2-0 win for Hearts. Incidentally, he also scored in the 1-1 draw when the teams met again on league duty at the beginning of December. Early in 2008, the striker moved to Viking FK in Norway before becoming a Rangers player for the start of the 2008/09 season, signing a three-year contract.

AN AMAZING JOURNEY
THE 2007/08 EUROPEAN CAMPAIGNS

It all began in Glasgow at the end of July 2007 and ended in Manchester nearly ten months later when Rangers faced Zenit St Petersburg in the UEFA Cup final. Prior to that showpiece fixture at the City of Manchester Stadium, Rangers had played a total of 18 European games on an amazing journey that had taken them from Montenegro to Serbia, then on to France, Spain and Germany before Greece, Germany (again), Portugal and, finally, Italy.

PART 1 : THE CHAMPIONS LEAGUE

Walter Smith's side defeated FK Zeta of Montenegro 3-0 on aggregate in the first of their two Champions League qualifying hurdles with David Weir and Lee McCulloch scoring at Ibrox before DaMarcus Beasley netted the only goal of the return leg game in a rather hot capital city of Podgorica one week later.

An altogether tougher proposition in the shape of Red Star (Belgrade) now stood between the Light Blues and the more prestigious and financially rewarding stage of the competition. Substitute Nacho Novo's priceless last minute goal in Glasgow meant that the subsequent battling 0-0 draw in the sweltering Marakana (where Allan McGregor would just not be beaten) was enough to guarantee Rangers continued involvement in the world's richest club tournament.

Drawn in Group E, Rangers emerged alongside Catalan giants Barcelona (winners of the competition in 2006) and the champions of France and Germany - Lyon and VfB Stuttgart respectively. Hardly surprisingly, this was immediately dubbed the 'Group of Death' in more than one publication.

In the first game, Bundesliga title-holders Stuttgart took the lead at Ibrox in the second half when Barry Ferguson was off the park being stitched (for a head wound) but Charlie Adam equalised with a classy right foot strike following Alan Hutton's lung-bursting, weaving run at the visiting defence. Jean-Claude Darcheville then hit the winner from the penalty spot after another surging run by Hutton was illegally halted in the box. As the stadium rocked, Manager Walter Smith wasn't the only one smiling that night.

Then, at the Stade Gerland in France, Rangers achieved one of the greatest-ever European results in the history of the Club after defeating Lyon 3-0 in their own backyard. As an added bonus, each goal was quite sublime. Lee McCulloch's opener in the first forty-five (a vicious Glasgow kiss of a header from Beasley's superb corner) was followed by second half strikes from Daniel Cousin (a bullet right foot drive after turning defender Anderson in the box) and Beasley after the wee winger took advantage of Cousin's long, pinpoint pass to coolly steer home past Vercoutre in goal.

Although Rangers held group favourites Barcelona to a 0-0 draw at Ibrox, Henry, Ronaldinho and co were at their brilliant best in the Nou Camp two weeks later and deservedly won. Goals from Henry and Messi helped ensure a 2-0 victory. Nevertheless, with two games still to play, Rangers occupied second spot in the group but Lyon's win away to Stuttgart meant that the French side's total of six points was now only one less than Rangers tally of seven.

Despite creating match-winning opportunities in the Gottlieb Daimler Stadium against Stuttgart – indeed the lead was taken courtesy of substitute Charlie Adam's close strike in the first period – the Light Blues succumbed to a 3-2 defeat in the automotive capital of Germany. This reversal meant that Rangers passage into the final 16 of the competition hinged on a winner-take-all clash with Lyon two weeks later.

On the night, however, it was an impressive Lyon who took the prize following their decisive 3-0 Ibrox win. Although Jean-Claude Darcheville missed a golden opportunity to equalise, Benzema's subsequent double more than ensured his side's progress in the competition.

Walter Smith's newly-built Rangers side could certainly be proud of their achievements on the 2007/08 Champions League stage and it will be a very long time indeed before anyone forgets that earlier (October) clash with the champions of France – the night Rangers roared defiantly in Europe to become the Lions of Lyon.

"Rangers achieved one of the greatest-ever European results in the history of the club after defeating Lyon 3-0 in their own backyard."

European Cup Winners' Cup
Winners: 1972
Runners-up: 1961, 1967

UEFA Cup
Runners-up: 2008

Scottish League Championship
1891, 1899, 1900, 1901, 1902, 1911, 1912, 1913, 1918, 1920, 1921,
1923, 1924, 1925, 1927, 1928, 1929, 1930, 1931, 1933, 1934, 1935,
1937, 1939, 1947, 1949, 1950, 1953, 1956, 1957, 1959, 1961, 1963,
1964, 1975, 1976, 1978, 1987, 1989, 1990, 1991, 1992, 1993, 1994,
1995, 1996, 1997, 1999, 2000, 2003, 2005

Scottish Cup (32)
1894, 1897, 1898, 1903, 1928, 1930, 1932, 1934, 1935, 1936, 1948,
1949, 1950, 1953, 1960, 1962, 1963, 1964, 1966, 1973, 1976, 1978,
1979, 1981, 1992, 1993, 1996, 1999, 2000, 2002, 2003, 2008

Scottish League Cup (25)
1946/47, 1948/49, 1960/61, 1961/62, 1963/64, 1964/65, 1970/71,
1975/76, 1977/78, 1978/79, 1981/82, 1983/84, 1984/85, 1986/87,
1987/88, 1988/89, 1990/91, 1992/93, 1993/94, 1996/97, 1998/99,
2001/02, 2002/03, 2004/05, 2007/08

Record Ibrox Attendance
118,730 v Celtic, League Division One, January 2, 1939
Record League Victory
10-0 v Hibernian, December 24, 1898
Record Victories
13-0 v Possilpark, Scottish Cup, October 6, 1877
13-0 v Uddingston, Scottish Cup, November 10, 1877
13-0 v Kelvinside, Scottish Cup, September 28, 1889

Q: SO YOU THINK YOU KNOW THE RANGERS!

1. How many trophies did Rangers win during Walter Smith's time as Manager of the Club from 1991 to 1998?

2. Name the scorers in Barcelona when Rangers defeated Moscow Dynamo to lift the European Cup Winners' Cup in 1972.

3. Who was the first foreign player to Captain the Club to a league title?

4. When did Rangers become the first Scottish side to win the domestic treble of League Championship, Scottish Cup and League Cup?

5. Who was the first Englishman to be voted Player of the Year by the Scottish Football Writers' Association?

6. An oil portrait of which legendary player takes pride of place above the marble staircase inside the main entrance at Ibrox?

7. With its imposing red brick façade, the magnificent Main Stand (a listed building as of 1980) was officially opened when?

8. He is the only player at the Club to have 'won' three separate trebles – in 1963/64, 1975/76 and 1977/78.
Can you name the legend?

9. One of his most famous goals was a blistering thirty yard free-kick against Celtic in January 1997. Name the modern great.

10. Manager Bill Struth once famously said 'Let the others come after us. We welcome the chase.' Do you know how many league championships he guided the Club to during his term in office?

U19s : at the double again!

At Hampden in late April 2008, Rangers Under-19 side defeated Celtic 3-1 in the SFA Youth Cup final. This victory confirmed the double for Billy Kirkwood's young side since, just one week before, the League Championship had been secured at Murray Park following a 0-0 draw with Motherwell. The youngsters had now completed this domestic double in successive seasons, having also lifted both trophies in 2006/07.

Last season, Rangers performed quite exceptionally throughout both campaigns. Indeed, prior to being confirmed champions, the side had lost only one league game – a 3-1 reversal away to Hearts – before going on an unbeaten run from mid-September until the aforementioned Motherwell clash in April. Along the way, impressive 5-0 victories were recorded over both St Mirren (away) and Inverness CT (home) in addition to a 5-1 win against Aberdeen and a 4-2 'revenge' win at Murray Park when the youngsters of Hearts visited in February.

The Scottish Cup road to Hampden began with a 12-0 rout over Fraserburgh in November and continued in much the same vein with Whitehill Welfare suffering 11-0 the following February. In the fifth round, it was altogether tougher opposition in the shape of Hearts (who lost 1-0 at Riccarton) before Dundee United fell 3-1 at the semi-final stage played at Tannadice. Incidentally, cup final opponents Celtic had disposed of Partick Thistle, Motherwell, Hibernian and Aberdeen before the showdown with their greatest rivals at the National Stadium.

With no goals in the first half, it was Celtic who eventually opened the scoring fifteen minutes after the break when Sheridan netted at the second attempt. That's how it remained until literally seconds before the final whistle when John Fleck equalised with a quite astonishing goal – the 16-year-old striker had run from his own half, brushing past three green and white defenders before unleashing an unstoppable left-foot shot from 18 yards that screamed into the opposite top corner. Into extra-time, it was advantage Rangers when Andrew Little, following an initial block by keeper Skinner, back-heeled into the net. Then right at the very end, as Skinner came forward into the Rangers box for a Celtic corner, Fleck broke away and ran 60 yards before slotting home into an empty net from 20 yards.

Even although this victory had not been as emphatic as last year's 5-0 demolition of Celtic at the same venue, it was understandably nothing less than another memorable Hampden occasion for the Murray Park youngsters......and that small matter of a double in consecutive seasons!

Goal of the Season

**Steven Whittaker v Sporting Lisbon,
UEFA Cup, Estadio Jose Alvalade, 10.4.08**

The icing on the Lisbon cake was surely this quite amazing goal by substitute Steven Whittaker. With Rangers 1-0 ahead and the final whistle within sounding distance, the former Hibernian man was calmness personified as he collected on the halfway line and proceeded to shimmy past various members of the retreating green and white defence before slotting past Patricio from inside the box. It really was an astonishing goal.

AN AMAZING JOURNEY
THE 2007/08 EUROPEAN CAMPAIGNS

PART 2 : THE UEFA CUP

Having parachuted into the last 32 of the UEFA Cup tournament, Rangers now faced Greek league leaders Panathinaikos who arrived at Ibrox boasting an impressive run of form - 19 clean sheets in all competitions so far this season and only a miserly seven goals conceded in 20 league games. Earlier in the group stage of this competition, the Greeks had comprehensively beaten Aberdeen 3-0.

A goalless draw at Ibrox was the end result of the first leg despite the fact that the Light Blues dominated and created the best of the game's chances. It was a frustrating night for Nacho Novo in particular who was denied on three separate occasions by in-form keeper Galinovic.

In Athens the following week, against a Panathinaikos side unbeaten in their last seven European home games, Novo was the headline hero when his late strike (from substitute Chris Burke's low driven cross) cancelled out Goumas' early opener to send Rangers through to the last 16 on the away goals rule. High-flying Bundesliga outfit Werder Bremen now stood between Rangers and a place in the quarter-finals of the competition.

On a night when Walter Smith's team formation (4-2-3-1 this time) was again spot-on, the Germans were

defeated 2-0 in Glasgow. Daniel Cousin netted the first with a speculative long-range shot just before the break that keeper Wiese completely misjudged. Then, right at the start of the second period, the visiting keeper failed to hold another Cousin drive from distance and the onrushing Steve Davis forced the ball over the line. It was the Ulsterman's first goal for his boyhood heroes.

For the return leg at the Weserstadion, Cousin was missing – he sustained a fractured jaw during the Ibrox clash - and with Darcheville still not fully fit, it was left to Nacho Novo to fill the role of lone striker. Right from the start, Bremen bombarded the Rangers goal but the defence (with shot stopper Allan McGregor irresistible and far more than just another brick in that solid blue wall) stood firm until early in the second half when Diego scored with a rather special strike. Despite almost relentless pressure from then until the final whistle, the Germans could not add to their tally although Ivory Coast striker Sanogo seemed certain to score late-on before McGregor denied him with one of the saves of this or any other season. In truth, from a defensive point of view, this had been one of the truly great European performances by a Rangers side.

At the last eight stage of the competition, the first leg against Sporting Lisbon in Glasgow ended 0-0 following a game during which both sides created few clear-cut opportunities. Incidentally, despite not scoring, the team had still achieved the best of all four home results in the quarter-finals.

One week later, Rangers 16th match in Europe this season was another extraordinary night on foreign soil for the club. Second half goals from Jean-Claude Darcheville (following a lightning break and subsequent superbly judged Steven Davis pass into the box) and substitute Steven Whittaker - a stunning solo run weaving past members of the green and white

rearguard - ensured a historic 2-0 win at the Estadio Jose Alvalade in Portugal. Walter Smith's side, in their first European semi-final since 1972, now faced Serie A giants, Fiorentina of Italy at the penultimate stage of the 2007/08 competition.

A banner simply stating - **THIS IS YOUR CHANCE. THIS IS YOUR TIME. BECOME LEGENDS** – was unfurled at Ibrox prior to the first leg of the semi-final and summed-up the thoughts of all friends of the Club that night. With both Barry Ferguson and Kevin Thomson suspended, the game itself ended in a 0-0 stalemate. Any real chances were conspicuous by their absence. For Rangers, progress to the showpiece final at the City of Manchester Stadium would now be decided in the Artemio Franchi Stadium, Florence the following week.

Defending as if their very lives depended on it, Walter's warriors kept favourites Fiorentina at bay throughout the second leg and the game finished with neither side having scored. Extra-time also failed to produce a goal. Faced with a penalty shootout for the third time that season, Rangers entered rather familiar territory and, albeit under far greater pressure this time, once again held firm. Nacho Novo converted the winner that took Rangers into raptures and to the final 4-2 on penalties.

An astonishing number of supporters - a figure of 150,000 plus was quoted - headed for Manchester in advance of the ultimate stage of the competition. In addition, some 32,000 fans gathered at Ibrox on the day to view the game on huge screens. Zenit St Petersburg, managed by former Rangers Manager Dick Advocaat, provided the quality opposition. After a disappointing first forty-five, Walter Smith's side dominated early in the second period but crucially failed to press home that advantage with a goal. Sadly there was to be no fairytale ending to this story and the Russians eventually lifted the trophy on the back of a 2-0 win.

Despite that night's disappointment, those who follow the Club had witnessed something quite special along the way. What began as an improbable dream had certainly come to an end but, in many ways, it was just the end of the beginning for Walter Smith's Class of 2007/08.

Home	Away
Rangers 2 Zeta 0	Zeta 0 Rangers 1
Rangers 1 Red Star 0	Red Star 0 Rangers 0
Rangers 2 Stuttgart 1	Stuttgart 3 Rangers 2
Rangers 0 Lyon 3	Lyon 0 Rangers 3
Rangers 0 Barcelona 0	Barcelona 2 Rangers 0
Rangers 0 Panathinaikos 0	Panathinaikos 1 Rangers 1
Rangers 2 W Bremen 0	W Bremen 1 Rangers 0
Rangers 0 Sp Lisbon 0	Sp Lisbon 0 Rangers 2
Rangers 0 Fiorentina 0	Fiorentina 0 Rangers 0
	(Rangers win 4-2 on penalties)

UEFA Cup final, City of Manchester Stadium, 14 May 2008
Zenit St Petersburg 2 Rangers 0

KYLE LAFFERTY

A boyhood Rangers fan from Northern Ireland, striker Kyle Lafferty was born in Enniskillen on 16 September 1987 and signed a Youth Team Apprenticeship with English Championship side Burnley when he was 16 years old. He made his first team debut for the Turf Moor outfit against Reading in Season 2004/05 and scored his first senior goal that same year in a clash with Luton Town. In Season 2005/06, Lafferty was loaned to Darlington where his nine appearances resulted in three goals. At international level his form was impressive, and during Northern Ireland's Euro 2008 qualifying campaign, he netted in the 4-1 win away to Liechtenstein before scoring the second half equaliser in Solna when Sweden were held in a 1-1 draw. Then, in a March 2008 friendly, the 6ft 4 hitman struck twice to claim a brace in the 4-1 victory over Georgia. He has signed a five-year contract with the Light Blues and gives Walter Smith a different option in attack.

MADJID BOUGHERRA

French-born Algerian international defender Madjid Bougherra arrived from Charlton Athletic in a £2.5m deal prior to the start of Season 2008/09. Equally at home in the centre of defence or filling the midfield anchor role, Bougherra joined Paul Sturrock's Sheffield Wednesday in May 2006 after an impressive six month on-loan period (from French club FC Gueugnon) with Championship rivals Crewe Alexandra. The player made an immediate impact at Hillsborough and won the Player of the Month award in only his second month at the club. In addition to captaining the club for the first time against Queens Park Rangers in October 2006, Bougherra also scored twice in the first half of that 2006/07 campaign. Although linked with several Premier League clubs during the January 2007 transfer window, the player decided to remain in the Championship and joined Charlton for £2.5m that same month. Then, when it seemed as if he was on his way to Premiership newcomers West Bromwich Albion in late July 2008, Bougherra signed a four-year deal with Rangers.

Rangers signed Portuguese midfielder Pedro Mendes from Portsmouth for £3 million in August 2008 and the 29-year-old made an immediate impact by picking up the Man of the Match award on his debut against Hearts.

Mendes, a Champions League winner with Porto, also enjoyed a successful spell at Tottenham in the English Premiership and as the Annual went to press Rangers were in negotiations to sign Major League Soccer star Maurice Edu from Toronto.

The Light Blues also snapped up Valencia midfielder Aaron Niguez Esclapez in August 2008 - the 19-year-old Spaniard, known as Aaron, has agreed a two-year loan move to Ibrox and the Club has the option to purchase the player after that.

Nacho Novo v Red Star (Ibrox, 14.8.07)

Second half substitute Nacho Novo's last minute goal against Red Star (Belgrade) in the Champions League qualifying round was priceless because in addition to ensuring a 1-0 victory on the night, it also guaranteed progress (following a battling 0-0 draw two weeks later in the steamy cauldron of the Marakana) into the financially lucrative group-stage of the competition.

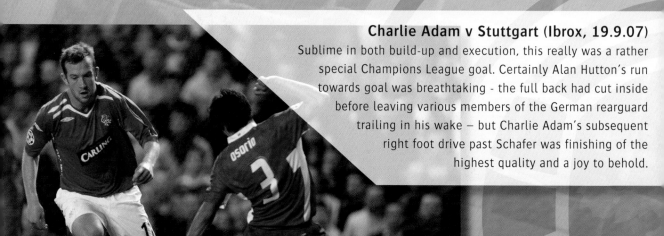

Charlie Adam v Stuttgart (Ibrox, 19.9.07)

Sublime in both build-up and execution, this really was a rather special Champions League goal. Certainly Alan Hutton's run towards goal was breathtaking - the full back had cut inside before leaving various members of the German rearguard trailing in his wake – but Charlie Adam's subsequent right foot drive past Schafer was finishing of the highest quality and a joy to behold.

Lee McCulloch v Lyon (Stade Garland, 2.10.07)

In truth, any one of Rangers three magnificent goals away to Lyon in the Champions League could make the top ten! That night's opener, on paper, certainly seemed relatively straightforward – a Lee McCulloch header from a DaMarcus Beasley corner. Cast your mind back, however, to recall the pinpoint accuracy of Beasley's ball into the box and the astonishing power of McCulloch's unstoppable bullet header.

Nacho Novo v Celtic (Ibrox, 20.10.07)

Ghosting between Caldwell and O'Dea, Nacho Novo's opener in the first Old Firm clash of the season was a diving header past Boruc that set Rangers on the path to a crucial 3-0 win. For good measure, the gallus little Spaniard (in only SPL start number two for the season) claimed his second of the afternoon from the penalty spot late on as Walter Smith's men joined Celtic at the top of the SPL table on 22 points.

Nacho Novo v Panathinaikos (Apostolos Nikolaidis, 21.2.08)

In Athens, with Panathinaikos leading 1-0 on aggregate and less than ten minutes of play remaining, Rangers seemed to be heading for the UEFA Cup exit door. That all changed when Nacho Novo, after being set up by winger Chris Burke, fired home from close range to secure the scoring draw that was enough to take Rangers through to the last sixteen of the 2007/08 competition.

Kevin Thomson v Celtic (Ibrox, 29.3.08)

Midfielder Kevin Thomson's first-ever goal for Rangers was also the winning strike in the second Old Firm clash of the campaign - not a bad combination at all. With the first half drawing to a close, Jean-Claude Darcheville and Thomson combined most effectively on the edge of the Celtic box before the midfielder, darting down the inside right channel, slotted home a cool right foot finish below Boruc.

Kris Boyd v Dundee United (Hampden, 6.4.08)

Drastic action was required as Dundee United led 1-0 with the Hampden clock confirming barely ten minutes to go in the CIS Insurance Cup final. Step forward substitute Kris Boyd who, five minutes later, drew Rangers level with an emphatic finish after capitalising on a defensive error. His afternoon's work still not done, Boyd's subsequent hat-trick would include the winning penalty in a dramatic shootout.

Jean-Claude Darcheville v Sporting Lisbon (Estadio Jose Alvalade, 10.4.08)

Following the 0-0 UEFA Cup draw at Ibrox, Rangers knew that not scoring in Portugal was never an option. In the event, Walter Smith's seasoned travellers struck twice, with Jean-Claude Darcheville netting the first of that night's glorious double. A Steve Davis burst down the right was matched stride for stride through the middle by the Frenchman who clinically despatched into the net from close range.

Barry Ferguson v Motherwell (Ibrox, 7.5.08)

With Rangers and Celtic still neck and neck in the race to be crowned champions of the SPL, Motherwell provided the opposition in the penultimate home game last season. There was only one goal that night – and it was a beauty! Deep into the second period, in a crowded penalty area following a Steve Davis corner, Barry Ferguson's control and finish left nothing to be desired as his hook shot soared high into the far corner.

Kris Boyd v Queen of the South (Hampden, 24.5.08)

Although both of Kris Boyd's goals on Scottish Cup final day were special, his first that sunny afternoon was really special. Following a foul on DaMarcus Beasley 22 yards from goal, Barry Ferguson just poked the resultant free-kick to his friend. Boyd's subsequent strike was perfect and an unsaveable right foot shot rose all the way before ending its journey high in the left-hand corner of the net.

Goals from Kris Boyd (3), Lee McCulloch (2) and Alan Hutton (his last Rangers goal before moving to Tottenham Hotspur) ended the Scottish Cup dreams of Third Division East Stirling at the 4th Round stage of the competition.

Away to Hibernian in the next round, an absolutely enthralling tie ended a rather surprising 0-0 despite Rangers domination of the first half and the home side's subsequent control of the second period. Allan McGregor saw red late on, subsequently meaning he missed the Ibrox replay. When the teams met again in Glasgow, it was Rangers who created the better of the chances in another hard-fought encounter that saw substitute Nacho Novo sent off near the end. Chris Burke's super left foot strike from some fifteen yards shortly before the break was all that separated the teams at the end of the day as Smith's men progressed to the quarter-final stage of the competition and a home tie with First Division Partick Thistle.

A below-par performance against the Jags at Ibrox – the clash ended 1-1 after Kris Boyd had cancelled out Gray's second half opener– meant another fixture had to be added to Rangers already hectic schedule. The Firhill replay (in front of a virtually full house) took place three days after the UEFA Cup tie against Sporting Lisbon in Portugal. Following that night's heroic performance by the men in blue, Ferguson, Davis, Darcheville, Broadfoot and Papac were all given a welcome break. First half goals from Nacho Novo and Chris Burke sealed a 2-0 win. Although Kris Boyd never scored, he led the line quite magnificently.

Significant personnel changes were forced on Rangers for the semi-final against St Johnstone at Hampden as both Allan McGregor and Lee McCulloch had been injured at Celtic Park four days earlier. David Weir was also missing through suspension. Hardly a classic encounter, the game was decided following a penalty shootout after Nacho Novo had cancelled out McBreen's extra-time opener. Neil Alexander then saved two spot kicks before Daniel Cousin converted to make it 4-3 on penalties as Rangers booked a return date at the National Stadium in late May. Early on during the semi-final, both Chris Burke and Steven Naismith had been carried off, limiting even further the Manager's options at this crucial stage of the season.

Less than two full days after the side's final SPL fixture away to Aberdeen, Rangers lined up to face Queen of the South in the Scottish Cup final. The First Division outfit had, of course, famously defeated Aberdeen 4-3 at the semi-final stage of the competition. The first half certainly belonged to Walter Smith's side and goals from Kris Boyd (a thunderous right-foot drive that soared past keeper MacDonald) and DaMarcus Beasley (a low shot following Carlos Cuellar's looping header across the penalty area) seemed to have stamped Rangers name on the old trophy. Although two goals from Queen of the South changed the complexion of the game shortly after the break, Kris Boyd proved to be a cup final saviour for the second time that season when his super close-range header sealed victory for Rangers. It was the striker's 25th goal in just 25 starts.

After 68 games, 6360 minutes of football, three penalty shoot-outs and two trophies, Rangers marathon season had finally come to an end - just 297 days after it all started back in July 2007!

Rangers: Alexander, Whittaker, Cuellar, Weir, Papac, McCulloch, Ferguson, Thomson, Beasley (Davis), Darcheville (Fleck) and Boyd.

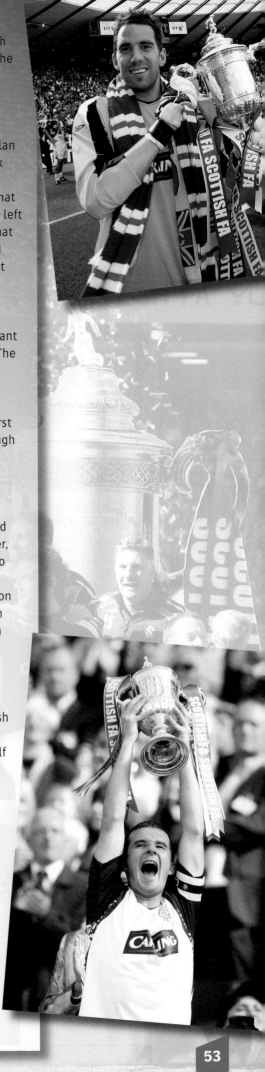

CAN YOU SPOT THE BALL?

ANSWERS ON PG. 62

CAN YOU SPOT THE 5 DIFFERENCES?

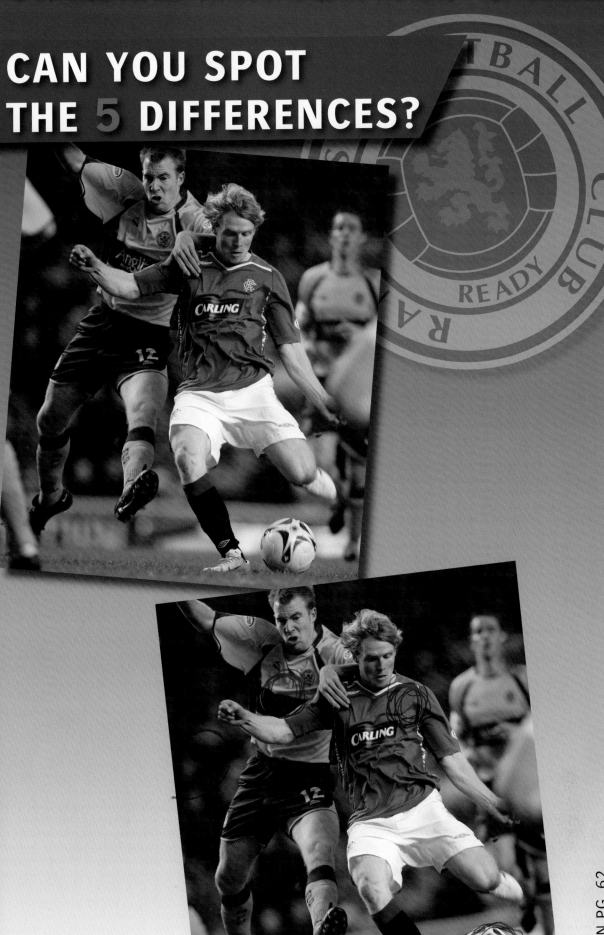

ANSWERS ON PG. 62

Rangers Annual
Player of the Year

Allan McGregor – joint winner

The road to Manchester and the 2008 UEFA Cup final was understandably littered with many memorable moments. Some, indeed, fell into the magical category. Near the top of any such list from last season would surely be what many considered to be the defining moment of the away clash with Werder Bremen – Allan McGregor's quite astonishing save from substitute Boubacar Sanogo. How he managed to turn that close-range shot onto the crossbar during Rangers defensive stand at the Weserstadion is still anybody's guess!

Under contract until the summer of 2010, McGregor signed for Rangers in 1998 but a wrist injury during a youth match curtailed his initial development at the Club. He eventually made his debut in a Scottish Cup tie with Forfar in February 2002. Seasons 2004/05 and 2005/06 saw the player on loan to St Johnstone (he was the first keeper to record six consecutive clean sheets at the Perth club) and Dunfermline respectively.

After eight consecutive starts at the beginning of the 2006/07 campaign, McGregor returned to the bench when manager Paul Le Guen decided to restore fellow countryman and his first choice for the position Lionel Letizi. However, after returning to the side in early November for the 2-0 win over Maccabi Haifa, the Scot was ever-present from then until the end of the season at which time he was honoured with the Rangers Players' Player of the Year award.

Last season, both home and abroad, McGregor was simply immense with a string of match-winning saves in a number of games. Away to Red Star in the stifling heat of the Marakana during the Champions League qualifying fixture, he would just not be beaten as Rangers held firm for a crucial 0-0 draw. His penalty save from Wilkie in the CIS Insurance Cup final shootout meant that Kris Boyd could win the trophy for Rangers with the next kick. At home to Celtic, his stunning stop from a fierce Hinkel drive ensured there would be no share of the points after Kevin Thomson's Old Firm opener.

Best of all, however, was that save against Werder Bremen on the night that the Germans dominated and had 18 corners, 10 shots on target, 23 off target with another nine blocked.

McGregor, of course, missed the latter part of 2007/08 following his injury in the Old Firm clash at Celtic Park in April. By then, however, he had done more than enough to justify the accolades that had come his way since the start of the season.

"How he managed to turn that close-range shot onto the crossbar during Rangers defensive stand at the Weserstadion is still anybody's guess!"

RANGERS
YOUNG SUPPORTERS

RANGERS YOUNG SUPPORTERS
BE PART OF OUR TEAM!

Join Rangers Young Supporters and get closer to all the action at Ibrox! Rangers Young Supporters is an exclusive members club for all Rangers fans aged 16 and under! The fantastic joining pack contains:

MEMBERSHIP PACK
- Rangers kit bag
- Matchday flag
- Crowd clapper
- Fun sticker sheet
- 5% retail discount card
- Club contract
- Birthday card
- 24 page newsletter – 3 times a year

Rangers Young Supporters are also entitled to some amazing benefits on production of their membership card including:

MEMBERSHIP BENEFITS
- The chance to be a matchday mascot
- FREE entry to selected SPL matches[1]
- 5% discount on Rangers merchandise in JJB stores[2]
- FREE entry to The Ibrox Tour with a full paying adult[3]
- The chance to take part in exclusive first-team events
- Discounts on fun and exciting things to do in and around Glasgow

PLUS - We're always working to get our members fantastic discounted offers, visit rangers.co.uk for more information

Become part of our team today! Membership costs just £9.99 for juvenile season ticket holders, £15 for UK and £20 for overseas membership!

CALL 0871 702 1972 OR POP INTO RANGERS TICKET CENTRE, RANGERS JJB STORES OR VISIT RANGERS.CO.UK!

Rangers Young Supporters: 0871 702 1972
Email: Broxi@rangers.co.uk
Visit: www.rangers.co.uk

1. Games selected by the Club, call the hotline for further information.
2. Discount valid in JJB Rangers Stores and JJB Stores for Rangers products only. Offer excludes sale items. Only on production of valid membership card.
3. Excluding school holidays. One tour per member, bookings must be made in advance via the Rangers hotline only.

Answers ???

Who said that ? (pg. 28)

1. French superstar Thierry Henry after Barcelona's 0-0 draw at Ibrox in the Champions League clash, October 2007.
2. Kirk Broadfoot speaking after the 2008 CIS Insurance Cup final win over Dundee United.
3. After being informed that Rangers had claimed their 100th strike in 50 games during the 2-1 win over Hibernian, Walter Smith answers his critics with a little humour.
4. The legendary Jorg Albertz.
5. Former Celt Craig Burley writing in The Sunday Times, April 13, 2008.
6. Assistant manager Ally McCoist speaking after the 2-0 Scottish Cup win over Partick Thistle and Stevie Smith's long awaited return to first-team action.
7. Former Rangers manager Dick Advocaat to Barry Ferguson after the 2008 UEFA Cup final.

Q: Headline news (pg. 29)

- Young players Chris Burke and Steven Naismith both star in the 2-0 win over Dundee United that took Rangers to the top of the SPL table.
- For the game against Dundee United, Barry Ferguson wore a special captain's armband with Motherwell crest in memory of his friend Phil O'Donnell.
- Rangers go seven points ahead of Celtic in the SPL after the 4-0 win over St Mirren.
- Despite rarely featuring in the game, Daniel Cousin nevertheless hit a magnificent winner in the 2-1 win over Gretna at Fir Park.
- Rangers 10th consecutive SPL win is courtesy of an impressive 4-0 victory over Hearts at Tynecastle.
- Werder Bremen goalkeeper Tim Wiese fails to impress in the 2-0 UEFA Cup Ibrox win.
- Allan McGregor's heroic UEFA Cup performance against Werder Bremen in Germany recalls the famous siege of the Alamo from early American history.
- Substitute Kris Boyd is the goal hero as Rangers triumph over Dundee United in the final of the CIS Insurance Cup.

Spot the Ball (pg. 54)

Spot the Difference (pg. 55)